LIVING

LIFE

ON THE

CUTTING

EDGE

You Can Make It

TIMOTHY LOWE

Living Life on The Cutting Edge
You Can Make It

By

Timothy Lowe

Table of Contents

Dedication

To my wife, Wanda, of 45+ years, I love
you for being by my side through it all!

Acknowledgement

To my four children, 18 grandchildren, and many others, too many to mention by name THANKS.

Introduction

There is no limit to your potential and success in life. The sky's the limit, and no matter what you face, I want to remind you that you can make it. My book is based on my life's experiences, coupled with indirect input from teachers, parents, children, neighbors, church leaders, and various military personnel. As you go through my journey, allow yourself to be inspired, knowing that you too can overcome obstacles with faith and courage.

1

Time Spent

There are people who we spend time with and in doing so, *they being whoever they are,* give us their best shot. So, we have to give our best shot to them because as we are looking to make it, we need to pay attention to those who are around us.

Sometimes we are not as focused as we should be, but that's the point of spending time to see what's going on in life. Where do you want to go in life? And with whom? There are people who want to partner with us, people who want to tell us things that are good and things that are not so good. Then we have to pick and choose who we're going to spend time with in our life, our daily journey.

We want to walk in faith, not fear because faith is a calculator step. We're looking to learn how that works for us. If we want to be an author, if we want to be a doctor, a lawyer, or anything like that, we want to be able to look at where we are, where we're going and who we're doing it with. That's going to give us the end result of what life is all about, what our purpose in life is, the aim and goal, and all that encompasses how our time is spent and if spent well with other people. You may feel alone sometimes, but that's just temporary, and it's not a setback. It's a set up. So, we want to be able to look at where we are, where we're going. I can't express it any harder or any more that those things are important, the people we spend time with are going to drop nuggets into our lives. We're able to take that information and turn it around for ourselves so that others may experience inspiration from us. Maybe not exactly what we're experiencing, but similar and be able to apply it to their personal life. Therefore, it must be time well spent and it will be. It will be well rewarded in the end. You'll look back and say, "Wow, I made it." But don't stop there, just pause for a moment, Selah.

Crossing the finish line is important.

However, the end results are well before you get to the end result. The indicators of,

- *Have I done enough?*

- *Am I doing enough?*

- *Who else can I contact?*

- *Who can make input into my life that will give me positive feedback?*

Some feedback may be negative feedback, but they are also growing pains, letting us know that, *okay, I can add this to the list, check that off the list.*

Then the X factor or something that wasn't even on the list gives additional inspiration and they think, *Wow, that person did that? I can do it too. I'm going to make it.* Therefore, the end result is going to tell me, *Hey, not only did I cross the finish line, but I've got another race to run so that I can be a positive influence to someone else along the way.* This will help them, their end results, having spent time with me pushed them forward towards their goals. Just like the people who are receiving this today, will know that time well spent with me, or you or anyone else, they are going to obtain great results at the end. The people in our lives are our resources, encouraging us to make it. Knowing this will make us happy. Be happy with yourself. That's the end result that I would like for us to get. Being happy with yourself is the ultimate goal.

2

Look-Alike

In the movie, they have coined the phrase, that says "Art imitates life "or should "life imitate Art?" Another phrase that has been said is, "Which came first, the chicken or the eggs?" It doesn't matter which came first, but I do know that we should emulate (be like, follow after, copy, do exactly like) our father (John 5:19-20).

People also say that when a man marries a woman and they spend time (quality and quantity) together, after a while they tend to look alike. To that, the truth is that someone may ask, "Is that your brother/sister?" We were conceived and came forth as off-springs of our parents, looking like them and acting like them, growing up into full measure with all the attributes that usually sustains us throughout our lifetime. Then, out of what seemed to be nowhere, someone introduces us to the word of God (which is Jesus). John 1:14 which reads, "And the Word became flesh and dwelt among us"; Jesus in the flesh He spoke, and it was so. The disciples spent time with Him; Peter eventually denied being with Him. As we spend that much time (quality and quantity), we can't help but be like or be "accused of" being with, being around, associated with that person. Associate pastors are "carbon copies" of the senior pastor, due to time spent and time served with them. Reaping what we sow comes whether we want it to or not. I've often wondered "what if," so I'm careful, maybe too careful to speak to do just anything. Ecclesiastes 5:2 states, "Don't be rash with your mouth and let not your heart utter anything hastily before God!" I know that we live and learn but let's not die and forget it all (as one of my wife's aunts used to say).

Our experiences aren't just for our sake, but sometimes what we go through (by our own hands or at the hands of others) is for someone else. Just like a lion may kill a deer, but a vulture comes along to enjoy the feast! Choose how you live and as a result it determines whether or not you have a happy or sad life. Joshua 1:8 describes it so well! Proverbs 4:20-23, especially vs 23, sums it all up! It's one thing to "say a thing" but to "do a thing," leaves a greater impression upon one's life! That backs up the saying, "Talk is cheap!" Can I walk what I talk? My mother once (or maybe several times) said: "Anything worth doing is worth having." What does that have to do with anything? Hmmm. We have because we do and do because we have. Man doesn't eat to live but rather lives to eat, so we must be at our best to live while we have a chance to do so. John 10:10 tells us that we should live an abundant life (overflowing, more than sufficient).

What do we see when we look at ourselves? Where are we going with this? What is happening in our lives that we are looking like someone else? Or are we looking like ourselves? We don't even know sometimes that this is where *I am*. This is what I need to do. And this is who I need to be. So imitation is a form of flattery when you imitate what someone else is doing. And it's like," Wow, I'm receiving this, I'm giving that and they're exactly liking what I do." So, art does imitate life and life imitates art.

We want to be able to just grasp that. What is it that we really look like?

From the very depths of our soul, inside out, outside in, nothing missing, nothing broken, what are we looking for? We have been given that mirror image to follow, either physically or mentally. It's not just what you look like when you look into a mirror like most guys and ladies as we either shave or put on makeup. What are you looking at? Are you seeing it? There's been times in my life when I was shaving and had to look around because I saw my daddy. My daddy has gone on to be with the Lord a number of years ago. However, I looked in the mirror and noticed that if I moved my head left and right, it was as if he was still there.

That was just an indicator that I look like my father. Though I may not act like my father all the time. Simply because we look like someone doesn't mean that we're supposed to do everything that someone else does. No!

Sometimes it's just the image that we project or that was projected to us. The same is true when it comes to marriage. If someone is married, after a long period of time, the couple will sometimes begin to look alike. I've been told, "You and your wife are starting to look alike," and others can probably attest to this as well. We have begun to mirror one another in our actions, we mirror one another in our deeds, and we mirror one another with the people who we come in contact with on a daily basis.

Mirrors help us to identify what's going on in our lives. When you can see yourself, you know what you have at your access, the quality and quantity to make it and that's a persona that I really can't describe. Except you just have to try it for yourself. As you see yourself, you make sure that you're well groomed, making sure your dress or your shirt and pants are straight, and your shoes are shined.

When I was in the military, we had to look alike. We all had the same color uniform. We all had the same style shoes and boots. For the guys, we all had the same haircut and the ladies had their hair up in a bun. They had to look alike also. That gave us a comradery, and it gave us a desire to push forward. We knew that eventually we were going to be able to break out on our own and we wouldn't have that same image. But when we do have it, it would help somebody else along the way, because then they have grasped it. We've got that gumption on the inside of us, that we do look alike and what we were projected to have or what we are projecting to do.

So, we've got to be able to take all of that and put it in a nutshell and hold it in such a fashion that we receive and give the finished product.

Let's just take a pen and paper and write down what we see, who are the people who around us? I have a neighbor who rides his lawnmower every week with Gusto. And to me, that's quality because he doesn't miss anything. So, in order for me to emulate what he's doing, *I don't have a riding lawnmower*, but I used what I had, *my hand mower* and I followed suit, doing what he was doing. It wasn't so much the quantity , but the quality of it, and that's the seal of approval that we should have on our lives. Our quantity is meaningful up until a point, like making money. You can only make so much, but the quality of how you earned it is the most important. The question is, what did you do to earn it? How did you get there? Quality means something because it speaks more volumes than the quantity. You can have a stack of money, but how did you earn it? How did you get this money? So quality is probably far more valuable than the quantity. We have access to both, but we have to be able to take both of those and balance them because that's what our lives are supposed to be about.

If we have too much quality and not enough quantity or vice versa, we're going to miss something, but it's okay. We can recover from that.

3

Abundant Lifestyle

Where is there? Is *there* at the end of the line? Not always. *There* is different for different people. I've been taught how to do the alphabet from A to Z. So, the end deadline is the Z. The starting point is A, sometimes you go A, B, C, and then you can go back to C, B A. Then you start taking the letters and mixing them around to come up with different words and different phrases and in doing so, you get there and find that there is in parentheses, I haven't made it completely. I've made it from where I was to the next phase. Sometimes those cross lines, you might take A and go all the way around the world and never get to B, or you may take Z and back up and go around or start with Z.

So that's what I say about getting to there. Where is there? What is in front of me? What is the final stop or is that just a pause and go to the next stop? So, we want to be able to just do it over and over again, until we feel a confidence and a comfort in our mind and in our heart. Then you'll have that aha moment, saying, "I made it, I'm there." Getting *there* is true abundance. You can have too much of one thing and not enough of another, but the abundance is the satisfaction that no one can take from me. It's mine.

Once you obtain it, no one can take it from you. And as an individual, you're seeking to make it in life.

We want to be able to do it in such a fashion that says, "Hey, I made it. I ran into some humps and bumps, but I've got that abundance, knowing that my lifestyle speaks for me and that no one can take it from me."

We are raising the standards. Setting the bar high, and some people say, "Reach sky high" but can you go out of that stratosphere into the next ozone layer or dig way deep?

I got a friend who plants in our yard. And she said that when she goes to pull them up, it's hard because they're all the way grown down to China. I'm thinking, "Nah, not that far, but it is deep." Nevertheless, sometimes things get hard. And so, we have to raise a standard up side or down, depending on which way we're wanting to go.

Let's use Gold Rush for example. Although I've never been there, the gold that people shop for, had to raise the standard of how they got there to get the gold. Sometimes they had to blow things up or they had to keep digging with a shovel. In this case, sometimes that shovel is our own mind. Sometimes that shovel is that pen, putting it on to paper to say, "I'm raising the standard so that I can obtain not what Joey did, but attain something different than Joey, or even greater than Joey." Not in a competitive way, but in a way that satisfaction sets in and you can relax and have that aha moment and say, *"Well, I made it and that's my right there. That's my lifestyle that I worked hard for."*

It's well worth being emulated. If you follow the pattern and do it over and over again, you'll be on your way. Even as a writer, write on that paper and ball that page up, don't just throw it away. Just ball it up and put it to the side and then go to the next page and keep going. You'll get a satisfaction knowing that you made it and didn't give up. It's not just a gamble to keep going in life, it's adding substance to your journey. Life is a substance. It's like faith, basically the substance of things, hope for the evidence of things not seen.

Therefore, we have an abundant life in front of us. But it's up to us to decide *I'm going to go for it.*

4

"Jehovah"

J ust in these few names of God (Hebrew) it's evident that we're to live an abundant life.

Jireh: Jehovah will see to it

Nissi: Jehovah is my banner

Tsidkenu: Jehovah is our righteousness

Shalom: Jehovah is our peace

Shammah: Jehovah is thither (here)

Jehojakin: Jehovah will establish

Jehojakim: Jehovah will raise

Jehojarrib: Jehovah will attend

Rapha: Jehovah who heals you

So, it is important what we speak, for in doing so, we eventually bring it (whatever it is) to pass because we believe it, it is studied and practiced to the point that it becomes alive! Don't let life pass you by. Find out what "it" is you're to do and do it. Take that chance of a lifetime! The opportunity is there and don't worry about making mistakes. Matt 6:25 typifies what worrying can/will do. But the other side of the coin represents what to do about worrying/making mistakes; just get up and go again or try something else (II Cor 4:8,9). It is said that "Faith is the substance of things hoped for and the evidence of things not seen." (Hebrew 11:1). This can be interpreted as faith being a "calculated step!" A very loving pastor's wife shared that with me. If one were to look at life in that manner, it's understandable how/why the "Father of Faith (Abraham)" was able to just go ahead with whatever God asked of him to do or to go, by planning and preparing. Abraham did just that, not worrying where he was going or how. To travel without any preparation isn't a calculated step, but one that isn't thought out to live on the cutting edge as shown here means that one need not look left or right, but charging the bull, head on (as a challenge one doesn't readily accept), not concerned about the outcome, but the right now. Matthew 6:31/34 clearly illustrates this point. I believe we spend (in today's time frame) too much time talking and NOT ENOUGH time doing! It's okay to dream, but I'm learning and convinced that if not put to paper and executed, it won't come to pass, thereby denying one to live life on the cutting edge or even appreciating it. Statistics state that man doesn't even use 50% of his brain. Seems unfair to compare us to Adam (first man) since he was able to use 100% of his brain power, naming every animal and plant. It didn't matter that he messed up or not.

It's important that we learn from life's experiences and whatever mistakes we make from birth to the grave, there are valuable lessons to learn from and not be afraid to continue on in God. Our life experiences aren't just for us but for others, others that we may not ever see. That's why it's important to be led by the Holy Ghost to pray for needs to be met and to be used of God. Matt 8:5-13 reminds me of the centurion who knew his authority lines, up to a point, but knew also that where he felt his authority lines ended that Jesus' authority picks up. Something about having faith, exercising it to the max.

5

Life Experiences

When one exercises his muscles, first it must be decided which muscles to exercise, and for how long and what is the expected outcome of the exercise. Applying one's faith is just like that, but also from the opposite side of the spectrum, the only result of that is results! Living life on the cutting edge is a force to be reckoned with, calculated or not, we must step out by faith to see things to the end, whatever lies beyond what we see, on the other side! Faith can also be like healing instant or progression. What we see isn't always what we see! So, with that in mind it would behoove us to be excited or afraid of the direction we're headed in, not knowing the outcome but expecting SOMETHING none the less! When we moved from Savannah Georgia to Indianapolis, it wasn't a calculated step (faith in full evidence) from what the external appearances told you. It appears we didn't have it together nor did we know what or where we were going/ doing- But, as II Cor 4:18 proclaims, we don't tend to look beyond but what is (at least we're always being led to look at things face value). But as II Cor 4:18 says we looked beyond what one could see in the natural and saw the super natural and we did know what we were doing, even though right up to the day we left, we knew in our spirit that this move was the thing to do. Sometimes we must go beyond the limits that are set, in order to get what we've never gotten before! This means if no one else goes or believes what is about to happen, you stick to your course. Romans 8:38 states it well – I am persuaded, that nothing can separate me from where the Lord is and how we're to get to Him. This is essential to live to the fullest, reaching up to a level that at times seems unreachable. It's when we stop reaching that we fail at the relationship, such as it is. We must be real with ourselves, because I'm a firm believer that in order to live life on the cutting edge, one must be real and allow all the nuances that comes with the real to have a dramatic positive effect. In doing so, we become transparent to the point that the REAL "produces the impact intended."

We gain experiences from others who have actually obtained it. In my life, experiences have caused me to realize that it's not just a dream. You're not dozing off. Stay focused!

We need to stay awake physically, mentally, and emotionally.

Remember that we're gaining something at the end of this. Keep on going. And the question that I propose that you ask yourself is, "Are you just a statistic?" As life experiences happen, some people may say, "Well, I didn't do anything. I did what my parents or my teachers, pastor, or whoever was in front of me did." That was their experiences. What about me? Don't just be a statistic. Other people have many experiences that they could have shared, but that's their life experience. Make it personal! Ask yourself, *What about me? What can I contribute and leave behind for others? What makes me unique? What makes me so special that someone else will want what I've got?*

Not that I'm selfish or that I'm the best thing going. You know that old phrase, the best thing since butter?

My mom was a contract specialist in Air Force, and I followed her career as best as I could from a distance. I said, "I don't want to be like my mother." But low and behold, little Timmy became big Timmy and wound up doing some of the same things that mama did. From an Army point of view, people said, "Wow, where did you get that experience?" Well, I watched and learned. That's what we have to do. Sometimes we just have to watch, don't talk, just watch. And then we can jot it down and go from there. Those are golden nugget experiences that will make our lives even better.

6

Transparency

The opposite can be said when you aren't allowing your true colors to be seen. In the book of Acts, the passage says that "In Him we live, move and have our very being." (Acts 17:28). So, in order to be read like a book, I truly believe that transparency is the way to go! It is seeing through yourself that this leads others to Christ, then "It's all worth it"! John 3:21 backs this thought— when you really look at life with this passage in mind, there's no doubt that being transparent will no doubt cause one's life to be a cutting-edge model for many to follow. Follow me as I follow Christ comes to mind at this point. (I Cor 11:1 and I Cor 4:16). So, are we really in our Heavenly Father's image through His Son Jesus (which is the ultimate transparency), or are we like our earthly daddy? I believe we are and can be both, but there is a distinction of the two, like drawing a line in the sand. Living life on the cutting edge, one truly must decide to perform at the utmost highest level.

Oswald Chambers wrote a book titled: "My Utmost for His Highest." We are made or broken when we do! This highest means that we go to the extreme. I'm reminded of a saying: "Don't be so heavenly minded that you're no earthly good." When we have our heads so high in the clouds or the reverse, having our heads stuck in the sand depicts this thought. We shouldn't run from the truth nor use it as a proverbial shield either. What I'm saying is, let God and every man be a liar, to the extent that He is Lord, or He isn't over every area in our lives/situations. I think back constantly on what I remember having heard about my parent's way of handling issues. One would be the aggressor and it appeared that the other was non-confrontational at all! I have found myself employing both techniques at various times, which in turn speaks to the "living life on the cutting edge" aspect. We have access to some things inherently, while other things are learned traits. One must learn to balance life. When these thoughts are put into proper perspective, it takes on a new meaning. Who we spend time with does take on a new light as to what we think, but how? There are many people who have been and are being mentored, resulting in a good or bad outcome. When one gets married, he or she should sit down with each other, taking a sheet of paper and write down the pros and cons (my pastor often has shared this thought). After doing that, we should work on our proposed plan/plans.

Over time, improvising or new techniques become "cutting edge" stuff. None of this takes away from what we as people, married or single have observed or learned. It is said that imitation has been a form of flattery. It's important to embrace both likes and dislikes with wisdom, for one can have a proper balanced life, married or single. This can lead to a very challenging and rewarding lifestyle! Several people who have a church background (and some who don't) tend to push a little harder.

7

DNA

L iving on the cutting edge isn't just hoping or wishing that your life would be better, but that ACTION = FAITH, and FAITH=ACTION! Our DNA isn't just what we look like (or who we look like), but what's on the inside, and then how we play the hand that's being dealt! That is what other people have affectionately described as "the rubber meeting the road." Talk is cheap, so put up or shut up! You must allow yourself to be put to the task, which makes it all worth it! So, that emulation does pay off, for as people we are looking for the end results: "Did I make it/Am I a winner?" Don't stop there, because there may come a time when you/I fall, but during that time, we must get up, brush ourselves off and move on. Recovery is paramount in order to be successful. DNA does play an important part in our lives, but we must not stop there. Fight that good fight: many a scientist, doctor, lawyer, teacher, police officer, author, mom, dad, etc., have fought to succeed in life, and each one has had to stop and ask, "What was the driving force?" Was it DNA (that inherited "stuff") or was it learned? There's another phrase for what DNA could mean and that is, *Does not Apply* or does it apply?

Conclusion – Both! In these times, we need to be for real, not as someone has said, "In a land of d-nile..."we make life easy or hard, depending on how we "play the game!" We can either duck the curve ball or catch it and throw it back. There's a scripture that says that if we are properly equipped then the "game of life" can be played and WON! Each of us have that advantage available.

Life is worth the living on the cutting edge, and we shouldn't allow "things" to dominate us! Going from one challenge to the next one, takes courage, grit, and determination. That involves accepting the criticism, no matter how harsh it comes! (an author friend shared this with me). When you or I look back after all the things that have been said or done, and you/I can see that somehow, we made it, SUCCESSFULLY, a huge sigh of relief comes! This will allow you to say, "I won," even when it appears that you "lost"! No long dwelling on this or that negative moment in life, for ultimately you/I gain the victory...living life on the cutting edge does mean something, something that no one can take away from me/you.

I don't want to hurt anybody's feelings, but I am not a failure. I am not a failure because I am reminded of that as Mama said, "You're going to be something, you're going to succeed!" And if I did make a mistake or do make a mistake, I am not a failure because the only way to get ahead in life is that sometimes we're going to fail, but we are not mistakes. And until I learned how to perfect my trade or my craft, there were mistakes, but I took those things and learned that I am not a mistake. I didn't mess up. Something happened. That caused me to go the way I did. I had to just take it and learn from it and move on. Don't just keep holding onto it. Be satisfied with what you got, but don't hold on to it because there's something greater coming and that Greater One lives inside of you.

DNA becomes more real, doesn't it? Looking back on where/how our mentor(s), parents, friends crossed the finish line, sinks in, maybe sideways...take a look back on how you have lived your life; selfless or selfish is a heavy impact! We can say that "I wish I could change the outcome of my life during those difficult times" but crying over spilled milk when the bucket has been knocked over, there's no going back! As one gets older, wiser and more experienced, we DO CHANGE! Our opportunities to "live life on the cutting edge," are always before us, if we only dare. Not knowing what others have gone through (behind the scenes), we can't even imagine how/that they made it over! WOW! What a revelation!!

It's not the "ultimate" that is being referred to here, but how one does get ahead. It would appear that we get ahead in life on the back/shoulders of others. There was a mentor, unknowingly, who stated that one has to incorporate the efforts of 100 others as opposed to "you" doing 100 things yourself, now that's CUTTING EDGE!

8

Not Afraid

Not being afraid to make mistakes for fear of complete failure will cause you to stall. One who has emulated others, over the course of one's life: parents, life coach(es), teachers, pastors, spouse, or even one's self, we would be sad that we didn't even try! Regardless of one's DNA (that inherited stuff), you really had/have it made, because you/me kept on pushing, until that moment: I ARRIVED! One shouldn't feel defeated because of not being able to pick/choose our DNA, but rather, look to establishing your own cutting-edge society! Each one's merits are just that- THEIRS! Do not feel like you have any allegiance to any one person, unless something in writing or that "gentleman's handshake!" The cutting edge thought here is very much apparent. No definition needed. Life offers us many options, but why not work towards "living until you're satisfied?" Life can be a bowl of cherries, just remember to spit out the pits!

A number of times we encounter "pit-falls" and "pit-stops," however, those roadside obstacles tend to give us a chance to breathe, regroup, relax or just think, which may lead to doing NOTHING! Once the batteries are charged up and you feel like you've had a chance to refuel, do as a lyric suggests: "You can get back up again, fit for the battle."

– Living life on the cutting edge!

9

Getting Up Again

In order to complete the journey/mission, it may involve a different route...pull into a proverbial rest stop, rotate your stock, complete the evaluation and get on with it! Life is truly about choices, whether we make the right ones or not, CHOOSE! You can always get back up again...a mentor stated something that may be considered profound: "When you try, you fail, SO JUST DO IT! Raisins didn't become that way overnight...Everything we do, starts with a seed! Authors, friendships, whatever life's calling/passion, they had to start somewhere... God so loved the world, that He gave...life as we have come to know, it started somewhere, inception, growth, etc... we may experience some bumps, humps, jumps, but through it all – SUCCESS! Reach that desired goal, GET BACK UP AGAIN!! Get the calculator out; count up the cost; do the research, before, during and after, so that that desired goal is met/obtained. Make sure that it isn't/wasn't just an infatuation...what's your cost?? One plus one equals two, or does it? Where do we draw the line, or do we? The cutting edge means that sometimes we leave the "excess film" on the copy room floor. A potter molds his clay: shaping, forming, pulling apart, throwing on the floor, then places the clay in the oven, and, "walla!" A finished product that is sitting next to, not noticing or thinking about the "leftovers," aka DNA, IS WAITING to be used also! At what time of space does one seek that seemingly unattainable career/job, relationship, etc. YOU CAN GET BACK UP, AGAIN! The direction isn't always clearly defined, define it, step by step...scientists, researchers, didn't arrive at their conclusions in one formula. Sometimes one must remove him/herself from the environment, finding another resting spot where the continuation and/or completion exists! Living life on the cutting edge isn't always going to be popular, nor totally comfortable...what's in your heart of hearts to do/be? Selfish vs selfless...what is the main theme of your life's story/project? We all NEED SOMEONE ELSE to speak into our lives, to realize that WE CAN accomplish that which often evades us! Here are some ingredients in life: purpose, plan, start, ending, the unseen dashes, slow or fast start, educational challenges, etc. What is your desired outcome?

We fall down, but we get up. I've seen commercials where senior citizens had to learn to get up again by pressing the emergency button that they wear around their neck or on their wrist. And if they've fallen down and need help, then they push that button and it says, "I've fallen, and I can't get up." Then someone comes to help them.

Let's take a look at that. In life we want to make it in such a way that, if I stumble over the brick, boulder, and fall down, I've got to know that I can get up again. Knowing that I can make it in such a fashion that maybe the way I was going wasn't meant. Falling can redirect you, I had to take a different route and try another strategy.

We can get up again and realize that we've *tried it*. Things may seem like they aren't working, but don't stop. Sometimes we have to hear someone tell us, *you shouldn't do that*, because they're looking at us and knowing that we can make it. But we don't see it. At times those stern talks may make us angry and frustrated. I remember even now as an adult, a person who I worked for gave me a stern talking to because they saw the potential in me and weren't satisfied with where I was at. They wanted me to know that I could go beyond that. I thought, *Oh, that hurts. I'm not doing what they said, I'm a rebel.* Sometimes in our rebellion, we find out that we fell down, but guess what? Get back up, brush yourself off and move on.

When we do that, we are not only following the leader, we become the leader so that others can follow us. Therefore, when someone is struggling in life, in their profession, just things in life, we can see the similarities there that reminds us of when we messed up, but guess what? I can make it beyond where I was to where I'm going.

Brush yourself off, get up again and go because life is worth it. The challenges of life tell us that once we've done this, we have to do a different strategy. It turns us in another direction, but then we have to allow ourselves to come to a halting point and say, okay, *here I am. Where do I go from here? I am the leader.*

Be positive about it. *I am the leader. Follow me.* Not only as I follow Christ, which is very good, but follow me so that others can see that I'm showing you the way, so you can become leader someday. I challenge everyone, Get up again!

10

Stay Focused

Question. Are you a finished product? I'm reminded of a TV show called *Dennis the Menace* and his favorite line as he talked to the next-door neighbor, Mr. Wilson. He said, "Heck no. Mr. Wilson." And to me, he had to stay focused because Mr. Wilson was trying to tell him something about life, but he wasn't listening.

I can relate to that because I was Dennis, I'm not a finished product yet, but it's coming. That show makes me think. *How do I know this?* Someone had to tell me, "Tim, stay focused." I had to learn how to pay attention to what's happening around me.

Oh, you're not focusing on anything. Our thoughts are sometimes positive and sometimes they are negative, but it's up to us to decide to listen or tell the thoughts to shut up. *I'm not listening to you anymore. That's not where I'm at. That's not my life. I'm staying focused on where I'm going. What is my goal? What is the direction where I'm headed so that I can have an impact on someone else's life?*

Sometimes we got to slap ourselves, metaphorically. Slapping yourself is taking a stern look at yourself. Look at yourself and say, "I'm not finished yet. I'm not tired yet. I still got some more mileage. So, I'm staying focused." If you need to change the shoes on my quest, that's another way of slapping yourself. Maybe I need to change my appearance, sometimes appearance means a whole lot. When you're doing a job interview, for example, some places want you to look just like them so that you don't see you, but they see themselves. And then there are times when we go in unprepared, don't be unprepared.

Stay focused, look at what is in front of you. Write your goals down, put it on paper and say, "Okay, step one, step two, step three? Then the end result is..." Get to the finish line knowing, *I am a finished product.*

11

Where Do We Go From Here?

I've got it. I think it wasn't a dream. Just because you got it doesn't mean that I can't get it. And my promotion doesn't mean that it's a complete finished product, but it also means that I've went from one level to the next level and in doing so, I'm reaping those rewards. I'm finding out that, it's a Woosah moment where you just go and relax for a moment knowing that, you're moving from one level in life to another one.

We're going to have those things where we go from one level to the next. Those are call life's promotions. But in life, the promotion is, that I went from a child to an adult, to a husband, to a parent.

And along the way, it seemed like a dream. It was once a thought, that, *I can't obtain this*. But the promotion was the satisfaction of making it. .

I encourage you, to not keep looking over your shoulder at past accomplishment, go forward. Sometimes we promote ourselves down, sideways and out. Don't be a fuddy duddy, meaning *I thought I made it and I don't know what to do with my life.* I was in the military and comparing that to what someone else did for a career.

I have two older brothers and they only went so far in the military. Well, I decided to do better than them and do 20 years. Both of my brothers did three or four each. I said, "I'm going to do what they did, even greater." The closer I got to it, I kept saying, *I'm getting out.* But my promotion came in the military ranks and I was rewarded financially because I hung in there and I did what I was supposed to.

The 20 years finally was the top of the line for me, it wasn't just a dream, although that's how it started.

I once said, "I can't do that." But something on the inner side of me said, "I got next." Yes, I was next in line to be promoted not only from associate, but to be the pastor of whatever it was. And now I'm a life coach.

Promotion gives you satisfaction. Promotion gives you a reason to help somebody else and be that guide in front of them and let them know that yes, you can make it.

Conclusion

STAY FOCUSED! What is unique about you/me? Curiosity and blind trust seem to go hand-in-hand... don't be so hard on yourself! Allowing others to speak into your life's work/passion, eventually makes a difference, which will cause you to realize that you're "LIVING LIFE ON THE CUTTING EDGE"! Selah

Okay. Be confident. It's personal. It's your story that you're telling so that others will know that they can make it because you did and not to be as a competition. But just know that where you start is not where you finish. Once you're finished, it will be worth writing down. And sometimes it's going to be a no name journey. Sometimes it's going to be something that, "Oh, where did I get all of this?" "What happened here?" "How did I get to this point?" What has caused me to be who I am?" Just know that you're confident of what's happening and that you leave out or continue on a high note saying, "Okay, here it is." Do what I do. This is how I made it. You can make it, but that doesn't mean being a copycat, but in conclusion, YOU CAN MAKE IT!

About Author

I was born and raised in Dayton, Ohio. My parents were John and Mary Lowe, and I have seven siblings. I went to Fairview High School, graduated in 1973. I then joined the US Army, where I served 20 years in various locations. I am married to Wanda L. Lowe, of 45 years, and we have four grown children. I love to write and read.